Meeting the Millennium

30 Activities for the Turn of the Century

by Elena Dworkin Wright and Alyssa Mito Pusey

Ellen Jackson, consultant

with illustrations by Jan Davey Ellis
from the book *Turn of the Century*

Charlesbridge

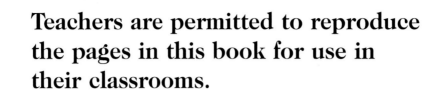

Teachers are permitted to reproduce
the pages in this book for use in
their classrooms.

Consultant: Ellen Jackson
Thank you to our Ghanian New Year adviser: Afari Dwamena

Charlesbridge Publishing, 85 Main Street, Watertown, MA 02472
Printed in the United States of America
ISBN: 1-57091-175-4
10 9 8 7 6 5 4 3 2

Table of Contents

On Time — Time Measurement

Once Upon a Time — The Last Millennium

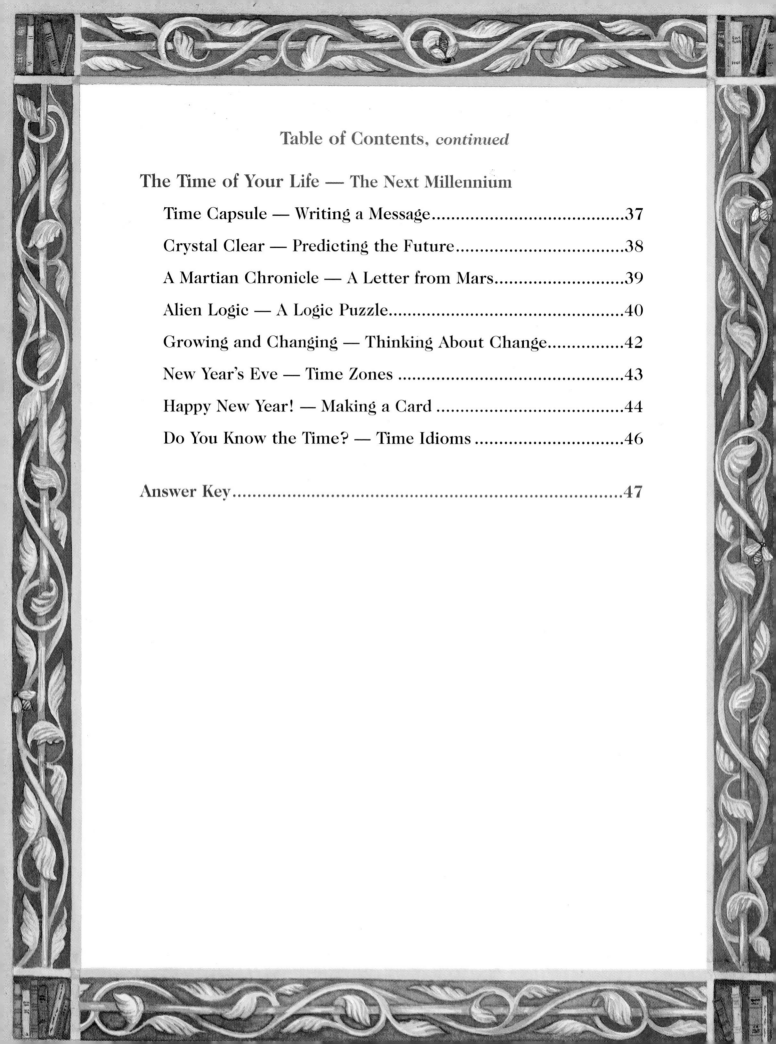

Table of Contents, *continued*

The Time of Your Life — The Next Millennium

A CLOCK IN THE SKY

Before clocks, people kept track of time by observing patterns in nature. One of these patterns was the changing appearance of the Moon. Every 29½ days, the Moon makes a complete revolution around the Earth. As the Moon moves around the Earth, we see different portions of its sunlit side.

The diagram below shows how the Moon moves around the Earth. A person on the Earth can see the part of the Moon that is within the dotted lines. In each empty box, draw what the Moon would look like to a person on the Earth.

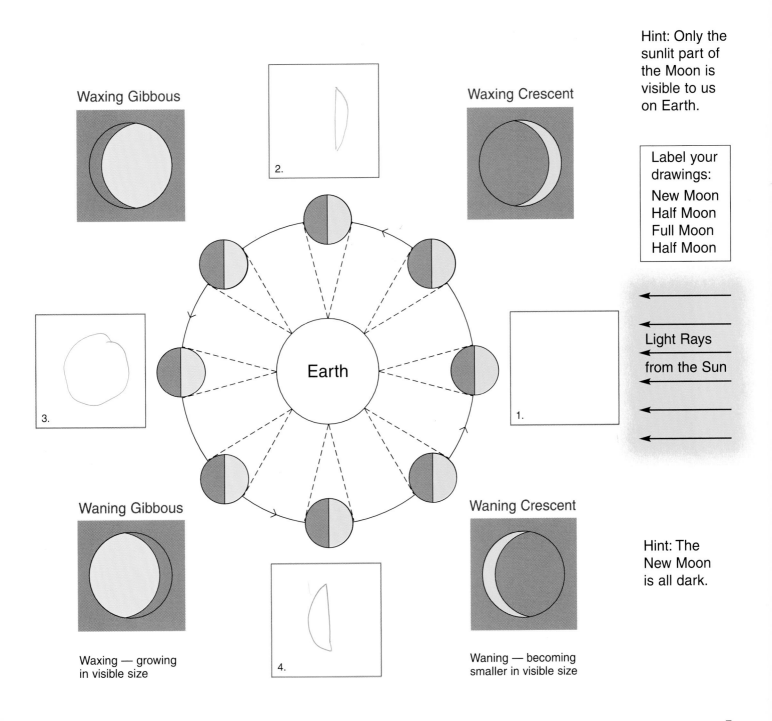

Waxing Gibbous

Waxing Crescent

Waning Gibbous

Waning Crescent

Waxing — growing in visible size

Waning — becoming smaller in visible size

Earth

Hint: Only the sunlit part of the Moon is visible to us on Earth.

Label your drawings:
New Moon
Half Moon
Full Moon
Half Moon

Light Rays

from the Sun

Hint: The New Moon is all dark.

THINKING ABOUT TIME

1. What is a clock? Write all the different kinds of clocks you know.

A clock is a thing that tells us when to do stuff three types of clock I know are grandpa clock, cookoo clock, and egg time

2. What are some "clocks" in the sky?

Hint: How did ancient peoples use the sky to tell what time it was?

moons, stars, and sun

3. What are some "clocks" in plants and animals?

Hint: Think about seasons.

spring baby animals are born, Fall leaves fall, and Winter snow falls

4. How would life be different without clocks?

no one will know when to eat or sleep

A Timely Thought

An hour was not always 60 minutes long. In the Middle Ages, people divided the day into seven segments or "hours" of equal length. In the winter, an hour was 60 minutes long, but in the summer, it was 150 minutes long.

TWELVE MOONS

Native Americans of the northeastern United States gave a descriptive name to each full moon. In this way, they kept track of changes in the seasons. The names used often varied from group to group and region to region.

Cut out the cards on pages 7 and 9 and put them in order to make a calendar. Write the calendar name for each month.

Strawberry Moon

Strawberries ripened on the vine in early summer.

Month: _____June_____

Flower Moon

Colorful flowers bloomed in late spring.

Month: _____May_____

Beaver Moon

Beaver traps were set in late fall, before the marshes froze over for the winter.

Month: _____November_____

Buck or Thunder Moon

Deer began to grow antlers; thunderstorms raged during this mid-summer month.

Month: _____

Cold Moon

As winter began, freezing nights grew colder and colder.

Month: _____

Green Corn Moon

The corn crop was ready to harvest in late summer.

Month: _____

TWELVE MOONS
continued

After you have put the moon cards on pages 7 and 9 in calendar order, you can use the cards again to play Moon Memory. To play, turn all the cards face down. The first player turns over three cards, trying to find the three months that make a season: summer, fall, winter, or spring. The first player to find a season is the winner.

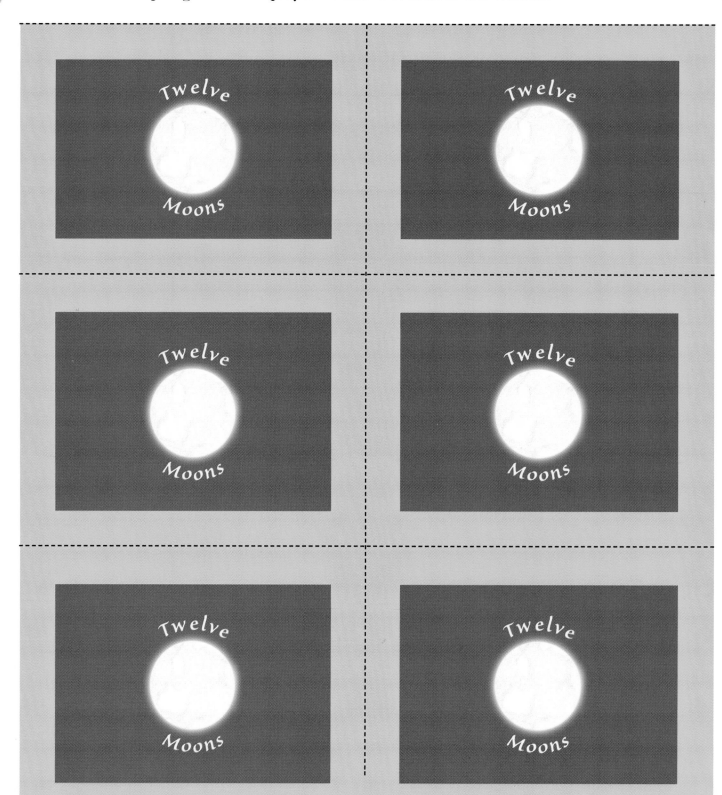

Cut out the cards on pages 7 and 9. Put them in order to make a calendar of 12 months. Write on each card the name of the month we use today.

Harvest Moon

Many crops were harvested in early fall.

Month: _____

Snow Moon

The snow pack was deepest in the last full month of winter.

Month: _____

Worm Moon

Earthworms attracted robins during this month when spring begins.

Month: _____

Pink Moon

Pink flowers blossomed in mid-spring.

Month: _____

Hunter's Moon

By mid-autumn, leaves had fallen off the trees, and game was easy to spot in the forest.

Month: _____

Wolf Moon

Hungry wolf packs threatened villages during mid-winter.

Month: _January_

Play Moon Memory using the rules on page 8 and the cards on pages 7 and 9.

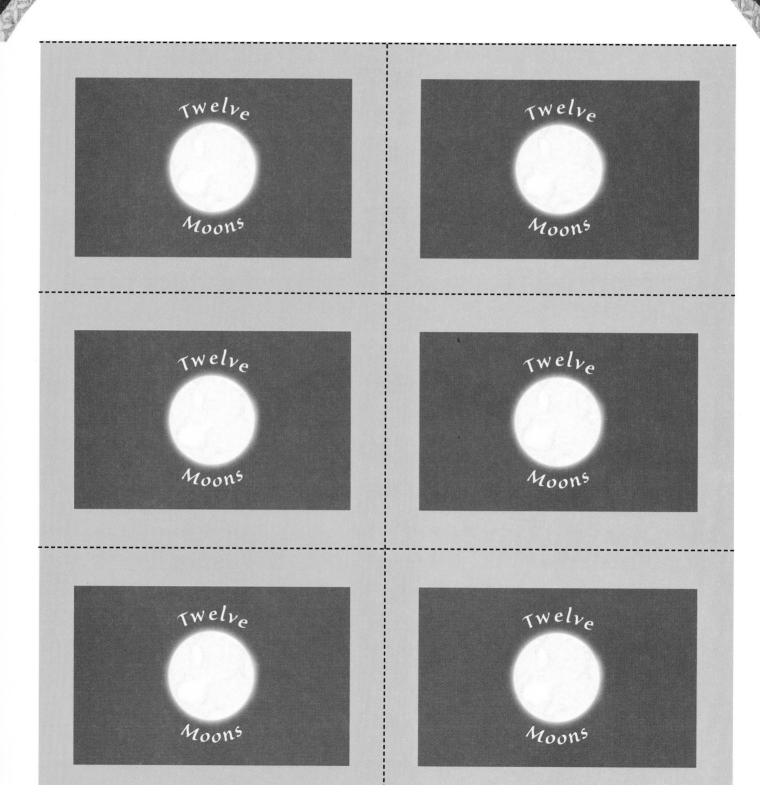

One thousand years ago, people used a different calendar. It was called the Julian calendar, in honor of Julius Caesar, the Roman emperor who helped develop it.

The Julian calendar had some of the same months that ours does. Can you figure out the names of the months from their Roman roots?

How the month got its name	Month
1. The name of this springtime month comes from the Latin word *aprilis*, which means "to open." In this month, buds open into flowers.	
2. Julius Caesar made January 1st the first day of the year, but most people kept celebrating the new year on March 25th. When March was counted as the first month, what was the eighth month? (Hint: In Latin, the language of the Romans, *octo* means eight.)	
3. This month honors Juno, a Roman goddess. Some people hold their weddings in this month, because Juno was the goddess of marriage.	
4. This month is named after the Roman god Janus. Janus had two faces, one looking forward and the other looking back. People felt that this was a good way to symbolize how we look back at a past year and forward to a new year.	
5. After Julius Caesar died, the Romans named this month after him.	
6. Augustus Caesar, the emperor after Julius Caesar, wanted a month named after him, too.	

HOW MANY MINUTES IN A MILLENNIUM?

Use a calculator to figure out the number of minutes in

1. a day _____

2. a week _____

3. a month _____

4. a year _____

5. a decade _____

6. a century _____

7. a millennium _____

How Long Is a Minute?

Estimate how long a minute lasts. Ask a friend to look at a clock with a second hand and to tell you when to begin. When you think a minute has passed, say STOP. Write down how much time actually passed. _____

1. Was your estimate shorter or longer than a minute?

_____

_____

2. How did you decide when the minute ended? _____

_____

_____

3. How else could you measure a minute without a clock? _____

_____

_____

FROM TIME TO TIME

You can make a calendar that lasts for 25 years. It will be good until the end of the year 2023!

Making the Calendar

1. Cut out Circle A below and Circle B from page 15.

2. Cut out the white areas on Circle A.

3. Use your pen point to punch a hole through the star in the center of each circle.

4. Place Circle A on Circle B.

5. Put a brass fastener through the holes to connect the two circles.

Circle A

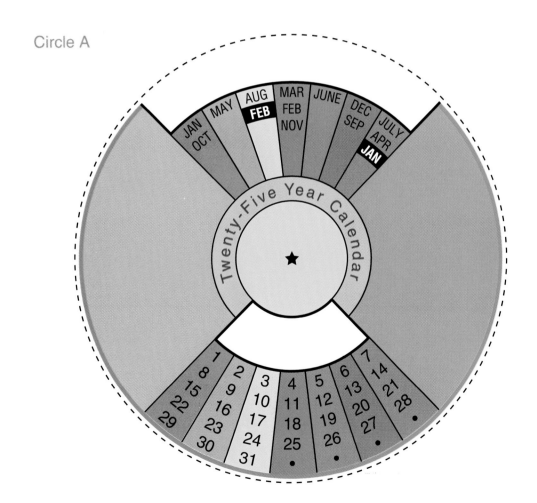

Circle B

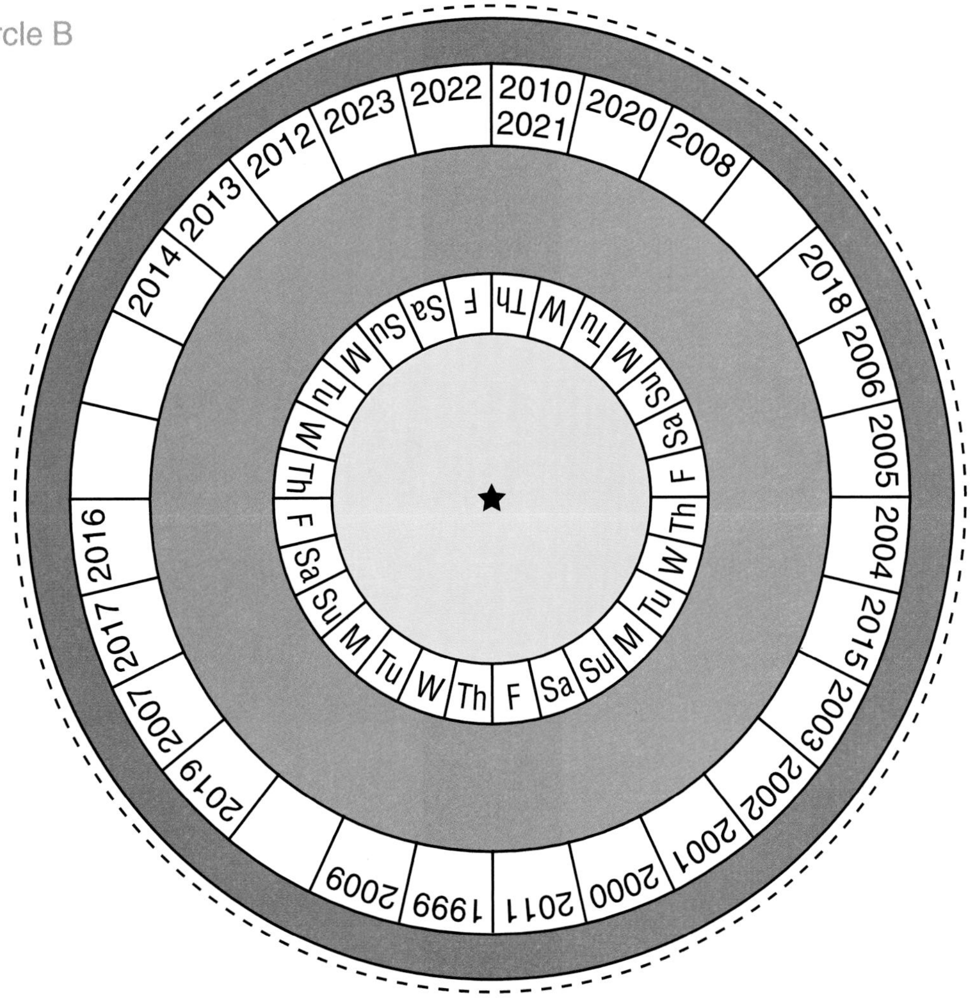

Setting the Calendar

1. Turn Circle A so that the year is over the month. If the year is a leap year, use the dark blocks for February and January. You now have a calendar for the month.
2. If you know the day of the week, read down the column to find the date.
3. If you know the date, read up the column to find the day.

Using the Calendar

1. On what day of the week does the last day of this month fall?

   _____

2. On what day of the week will your next birthday fall?

   _____

3. On what day of the week will you celebrate your birthday in the year 2023? How old will you be? _____

1. Use your calendar to find out when a friend or family member will celebrate his or her birthday.

   _____

2. Thanksgiving is always the fourth Thursday in November. What date will Thanksgiving be in five years?

   _____

3. What day of the week will January 1st be in 2010?

   _____

4. What day of the week will we celebrate the 4th of July in 2009? How old will you be then?

   _____

GEOLOGIC LOGIC

A millennium may seem like a long time, but it is short in comparison with the history of life on Earth. Life on Earth began four billion years ago. Humans have been around for only 100,000 years.

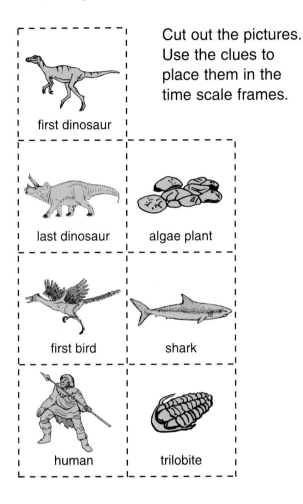

Cut out the pictures. Use the clues to place them in the time scale frames.

first dinosaur

last dinosaur

algae plant

first bird

shark

human

trilobite

CLUES

1. The earliest life forms were not animals.

2. Trilobites are an older species of animal than sharks.

3. The first bird appeared during the age of the dinosaurs.

4. Dinosaurs were gone from the planet long before humans.

5. Sharks are an older species than dinosaurs.

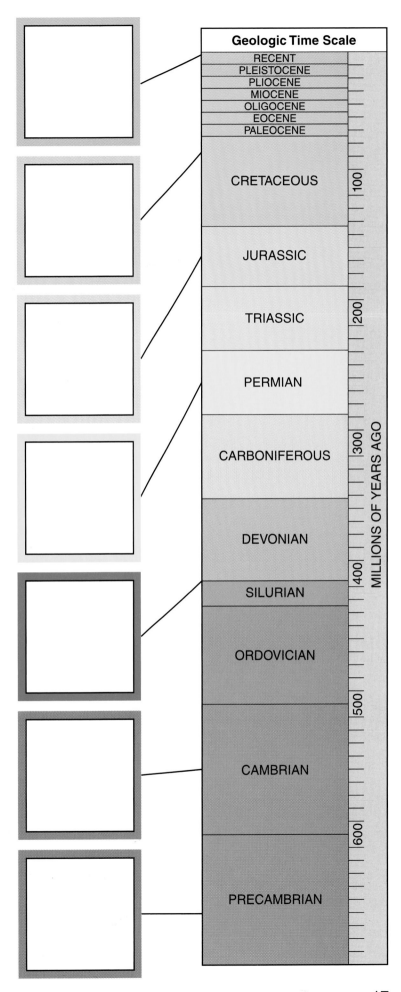

CALENDAR GAMES

Write the dates for the current month on the calendar form below.

1. Draw a box around a square 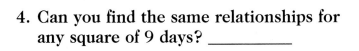 made of 9 days on the calendar.

2. Add the number in the center of the box to the numbers in two diagonal corners. What is the total? _____ Add the number in the center to the numbers in the opposite corners. Is the total the same? _____

3. Choose a different day of the week from each row of the square and add the numbers. How is the total related to the number in the center of the square?

   _____

4. Can you find the same relationships for any square of 9 days? _____

Sunday	Monday	Tuesday	Wednesday	Thursday	Friday	Saturday

ROOTED IN HISTORY

Why do people study history? You may be surprised to learn that historical events that occurred hundreds of years ago affect your life today. Every time you talk, traces of the past remain in the very words you speak.

In the fifth and sixth centuries, a Germanic people called the Anglo-Saxons invaded Britain. Their language is called Anglo-Saxon or Old English. It became the basis for modern English.

In the eleventh century, William the Conqueror sailed from Normandy, France, and defeated the Anglo-Saxons. He wanted Old French to be the language of the land. Old English and Old French existed side by side for many years, but eventually blended into the English we speak today.

Circle the German or French word that shares a common root with the English word.

ENGLISH	GERMAN	FRENCH
Milk	Milch	Lait
Flower	Blume	Fleur
River	Fluss	Riviere
Book	Buch	Livre
Color	Farbe	Couleur

In the eleventh century, people began to use many words with English and French roots. Write the modern English word that has come from each of the old words.

Old English	Old French	Modern English Words
Freond	Compaignon	*Hint: A person you like*
Wyscan	Desirer	*Hint: Something you want*
Rum	Chambre	*Hint: A part of a building*
Smull	Odor	*Hint: Relates to one of the five senses*
Andswerian	Respondre	*Hint: How you react to a question*

Many things have changed during the last one thousand years, but many others have remained the same. The following statements describe European life one thousand years ago. Put an **S** next to the statement if it describes something that is still true today. Put a **C** next to statements that describe something that has changed.

1. _____ Books were copied by hand and very few people owned one. Many people had never seen a book.

2. _____ Nine out of ten people worked on the land. Most people lived in dark huts with dirt floors.

3. _____ Boys were sometimes named Alfred, John, William, or Harold. Girls were sometimes named Alice, Sara, or Gwendolyn.

4. _____ People ate peas, oats, wheat, apples, pears, and plums.

5. _____ Most people believed that evil spirits caused illness. There were few doctors or hospitals.

6. _____ Farmers raised sheep, pigs, cattle, goats, and chickens.

7. _____ Both children and adults played board games, sang songs, and told riddles.

8. _____ People used sundials to tell time. Many did not know the date or the year.

9. _____ Many people never traveled more than a few miles from the village in which they were born.

10. _____ Men wore trousers, shirts, and belts. Women wore dresses or skirts and blouses.

FOOD FOR THOUGHT

Explorers of the New World brought back strange and wonderful foods to Europe. Sometimes, people were suspicious of the new foods. For example, they thought the tomato was pretty but poisonous and grew it only for decoration.

Write in the center of the web one of the foods from the list. Imagine that you have just returned to Europe and want to persuade people to try this new food.

There are many reasons why people try new foods: taste, texture, smell, appearance, uses, and nutrition. Write the reasons you would use in the boxes. On the lines, write the details to explain each reason.

Food List

Potato	Cranberry	Tomato	Chocolate / cocoa bean
Strawberry	Peanut	Blueberry	Squash / pumpkin
Pineapple	Vanilla	Corn	Chili pepper

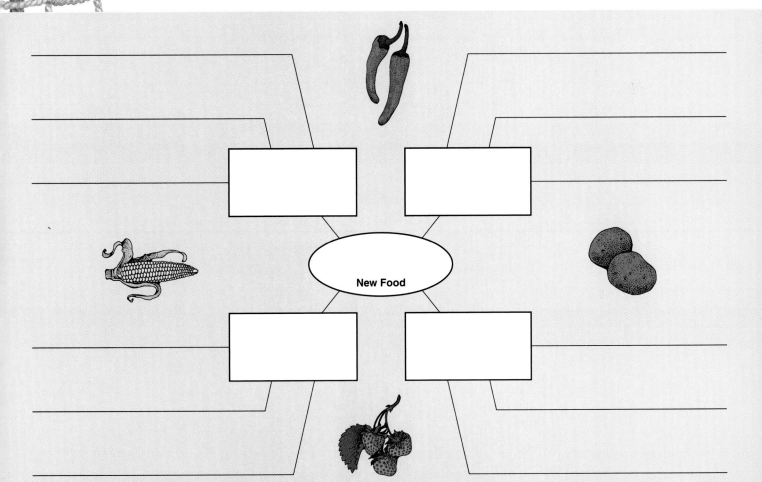

New Food

TIME TO EAT

Here is a list of table manners from the Middle Ages. Put an **X** next to those that are still important today.

1. _____ Bow to the gentlemen on each side of the Hall, both right and left.

2. _____ Don't laugh with your mouth full.

3. _____ Have your nails clean.

4. _____ Give the Porter your weapon.

5. _____ Don't blow on your food.

6. _____ Don't spit on the table.

7. _____ Don't chew on both sides of your mouth.

8. _____ Don't scratch your dog while you eat.

9. _____ Don't wipe your eyes with the tablecloth.

10. _____ Eat only twice a day.

11. _____ After meals, wash your face.

13. _____ Don't leave your spoon in your dish.

14. _____ Don't cram your cheeks out with food like an ape.

Until 1500, most people could not read or measure accurately. Recipes, like the one below, did not include standard units of measurement.

An Excellent Boiled Salad

To make an excellent boiled salad, take four handfuls of well washt Spinach. Boile it in water till it bee exceeding soft and tender. Then draine the water from it and chop it as small as may bee. Then boile it over again with six good lumps of sweet butter. Then take a good handful of cleane washt Currants. Stirre them well together with the Spinach. Then put as much Vinegar as will make it reasonable tart. And then with sugar season it, and so serve it upon sippets from a full loaf.

Imagine that you are a cook who must prepare this salad. Use the list of equivalents to calculate the exact amounts needed. Write the amounts in the ingredients list.

List of Equivalents

1 handful = 3 ounces

1 good handful = 4 ounces

8 ounces = 1 cup

1 good lump = 1 teaspoon

3 teaspoons = 1 tablespoon

9 teaspoons vinegar = "reasonable tart"

1 loaf of bread = 8 slices

1 slice of bread = 4 sippets
(Sippets are pieces of toasted bread.)

Ingredients List

_____ Ounces of spinach

_____ Tablespoons of butter

_____ Cups of currants

_____ Tablespoons of vinegar

_____ Number of sippets needed

25

Here at the nunnery we students rise in the middle of the night for singing and prayers. Then we return to bed and sleep until dawn. We spend the rest of each day in work, study, and prayer. Sometimes I help with the farm chores.

I already know how to fly falcons and play chess, but the nuns will teach me to read and write Latin, to draw, to embroider, and to prepare herbs and medicines. I hope my husband-to-be, Lord Norbert, will be happy with my skills. We have been betrothed since I was seven and will marry before I am fifteen.

In the Year 1100...

- Upper-class girls are educated in nunneries or in nearby manors, where they learn how to manage a household and to care for the sick.
- Parents arrange the marriages of their children. Girls are betrothed, or engaged, as early as age six.

Read about the education of Eleanor and Roger on pages 26 and 27. Then complete the chart.

Name	Year	Subjects	Availability of books
Eleanor			Books are rare. Only a few upper-class children are taught to read.
Roger			
You			

Today the bells rang at daybreak and we welcomed the New Year. I began the day by helping my mother make soap and candles. I cut wicks while she poured boiling fat into the molds.

At school we read from the **New England Primer**. We are learning to write a good, clear hand. Josiah could not do his sums and had to wear the dunce cap.

When I am older, I will be apprenticed to a silversmith. I shall stoke the furnace, sweep the floor, and learn to make teapots, buckles, and lockets. It is a trade that shall suit me.

In the Year 1700...

∾ Many people have books in their homes, such as the Bible and *Pilgrim's Progress*.
∾ Both boys and girls go to the new free schools. Business records and letters are handwritten, and it is important for children to learn good penmanship.
∾ Many boys are apprenticed at age twelve or thirteen. For seven years they are expected to work for a master while they learn a trade.

Use the education chart on page 26 to answer the questions.

What school subjects do you share with Eleanor and Roger? _____

_____

What did Eleanor and Roger study that you do not? _____

_____

Why do you think they studied different subjects than you do today?_____

_____

_____

What subjects do you study that Eleanor and Roger would not have studied?

_____

_____

I awoke at dawn. I placed a chair before the fire with a cushion for my lady's feet and pulled back the curtains of the bed, saying, "My lady, what robe or gown does it please you to wear today?"

I helped Lady Margaret dress, then beat the featherbed. I am needed in the kitchen this afternoon. Tonight I shall sneak into the great hall to listen to the traveling musicians perform.

When it is time to retire, I shall drive out the dog and cat and set the chamber pot ready. Lady Margaret is pleased with me and seldom pulls my hair. Though I cannot read and write, I do not hiccup, scratch, or blow my nose too loudly.

In the Year 1400...

- Girls, as well as boys, are sent out to work at an early age. Servants are fed and clothed, and it is expected that they will remain unmarried.
- Children have few toys. They play games similar to hide-and-seek and follow-the-leader. They spin tops, blow soap bubbles, and play with shells and stones.

Complete the chart. Then answer the question.

Year	Name	Play	Work
1100	Eleanor	Fly falcons, play chess, draw	Embroider, prepare herbs and medicines, help with farm chores
1400			
1700	Roger	Play with friends	Make soap and candles, learn a trade

How is your work or play different from what children did in the past? _____

_____

_____

NINE MEN'S (OR WOMEN'S) MORRIS

Ancient Egyptians, Viking warriors, English pageboys, and American colonists all enjoyed playing this board game. All you need to start playing are the board below and nine markers, such as beans, coins, or buttons. These are your nine men (or women). Your opponent should have nine markers of another color.

A mill

Rules for Playing

1. Take turns placing the markers on the circles. Try to make a mill — a row of three markers along one line. Diagonals don't count.

2. Whenever you make a mill, you can take one of your opponent's markers off the board. You cannot take a marker that is part of a mill unless there are no free markers on the board. A captured marker cannot be used again.

3. When all the markers are on the board, take turns moving them along the lines to make more mills. You can move only one space at a time (no hopping). You *must* move if it is your turn.

4. You win when your opponent has only two markers left, or cannot make another move.

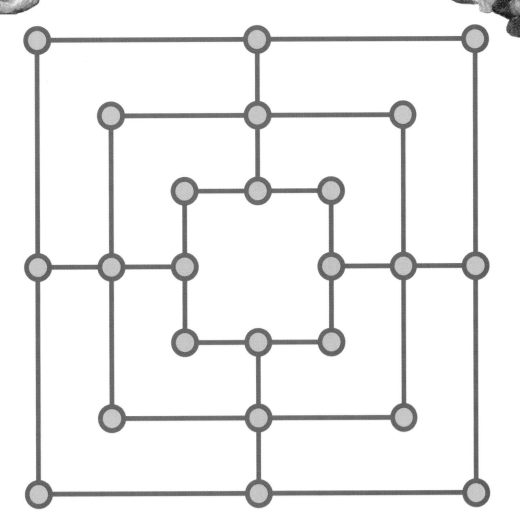

Look at the diagrams of clothing below. Draw a diagram of your own clothing in the empty box. Label your diagram.

cap with pearls

standing ruff

bodice

puffed sleeves

lace cuffs

long skirt

silk shoes

**England
1600**

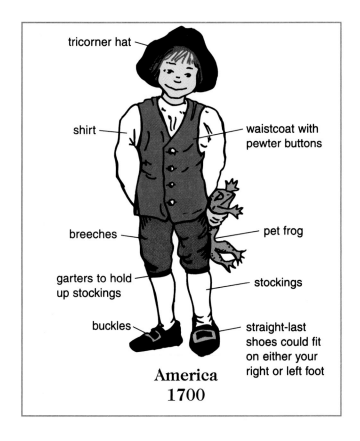

tricorner hat

shirt

waistcoat with pewter buttons

breeches

pet frog

garters to hold up stockings

stockings

buckles

straight-last shoes could fit on either your right or left foot

**America
1700**

1. How are your clothes similar to clothes in 1600 and 1700? _____

_____

_____

_____

_____

_____

2. How are your clothes different? _____

_____

_____

_____

_____

_____

HOMES THEN AND NOW

Homes have changed over the years. The picture at the top shows a frontier cabin in 1800. The picture at the bottom shows a city house in 1900. Complete the chart to compare the homes to your home.

	Frontier Cabin, 1800	City House, 1900	Your home, _____
Of what materials is the home built?			
How does the family get water?			
How does the family light the home?			
What chores do the children do?			
How does the family cook?			

IS THERE A DOCTOR IN THE HOUSE?

Read each column of the table.
Imagine living during one of those centuries.
Write a journal entry for a day in the life
of a doctor or a patient of that time.

	14th Century	17th Century	19th Century	20th Century
Doctors	Women cared for the sick. Doctors were rare.	Barbers not only cut hair, but also performed minor surgery and pulled teeth.	Doctors were available only in large cities.	Doctors are widely available. Many specialize.
Medicine	Mixtures were made from herbs, flowers, and other plants.	Mixtures were made from herbs, flowers, and other plants.	Vaccine for smallpox was developed. Ether let people sleep through surgery.	Vaccines and antibiotics are used to prevent or cure illness.
Average Life Span	20-30 years. The Black Death killed ⅓ of Europe's population.	30-40 years	At the start of the century, the average life span was 35 to 40 years.	By the end of the century, the average life span is 76 years.
Bathing	Most people never bathed.	People bathed only when a doctor forced them to.	Most people bathed infrequently. Being in water was thought to cause illness.	By the end of the century, most people in the U.S. bathe daily.

Date:_____

Journal entry: _____

_____

_____

_____

_____

GETTING AROUND

One thousand years ago, most people never traveled. They lived their whole lives within a few miles of the place where they were born. Now, many people travel every day. They zoom from city to city, state to state, or even country to country.

How did this change in transportation come about? Read the time line below to find out. The arrows show when people used each type of transportation.

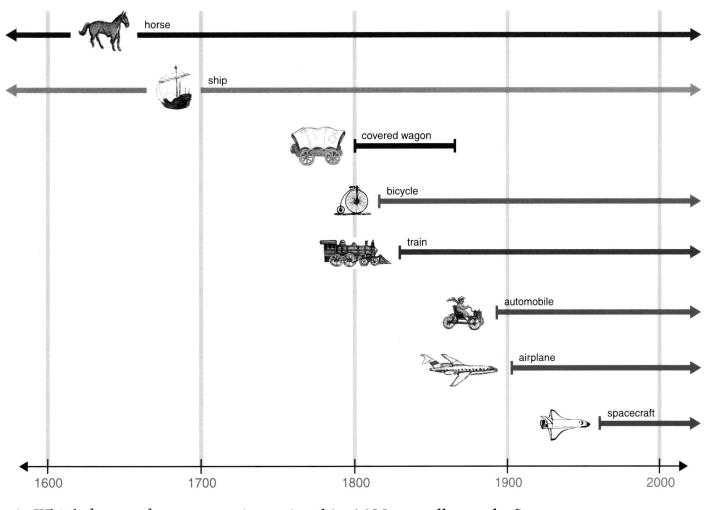

1. Which forms of transportation existed in 1600 as well as today? _____

2. When were bicycles invented? _____

3. How long have people been driving automobiles? _____

4. In what century did the greatest changes in transportation occur? _____

5. How do you think people felt about these changes?_____

_____

6. Which of these forms of transportation do we still use today? _____

_____

Choose one century from the past millennium. Find out who are the ten most famous people from that century.

Make a time line for the century:

1. Cut out the two halves of the time line on page 35.
2. Join the two halves by taping edge A and edge B together to make one long strip.
3. The strip of paper represents a century. Write a title for the century in the yellow banner.
4. Each colored rectangle represents the ten years of a decade. On the line above each rectangle, write the year when the decade started.
5. For each of the ten famous people, write an accomplishment on the time line at the date when it occurred. You can write above or below the colored rectangles.
6. You may want to illustrate your time line with pictures to show what the people did.

This is a section of a time line for the twelfth century.

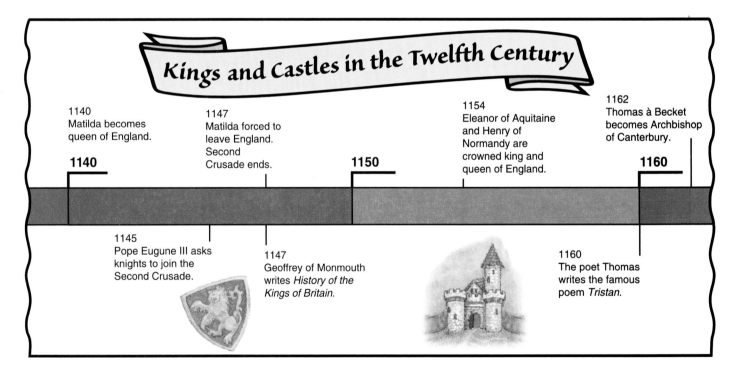

When you have completed your century time line, you might tape it to other centuries to create a time line of the entire millennium.

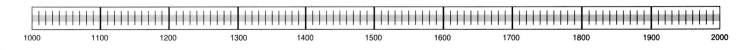

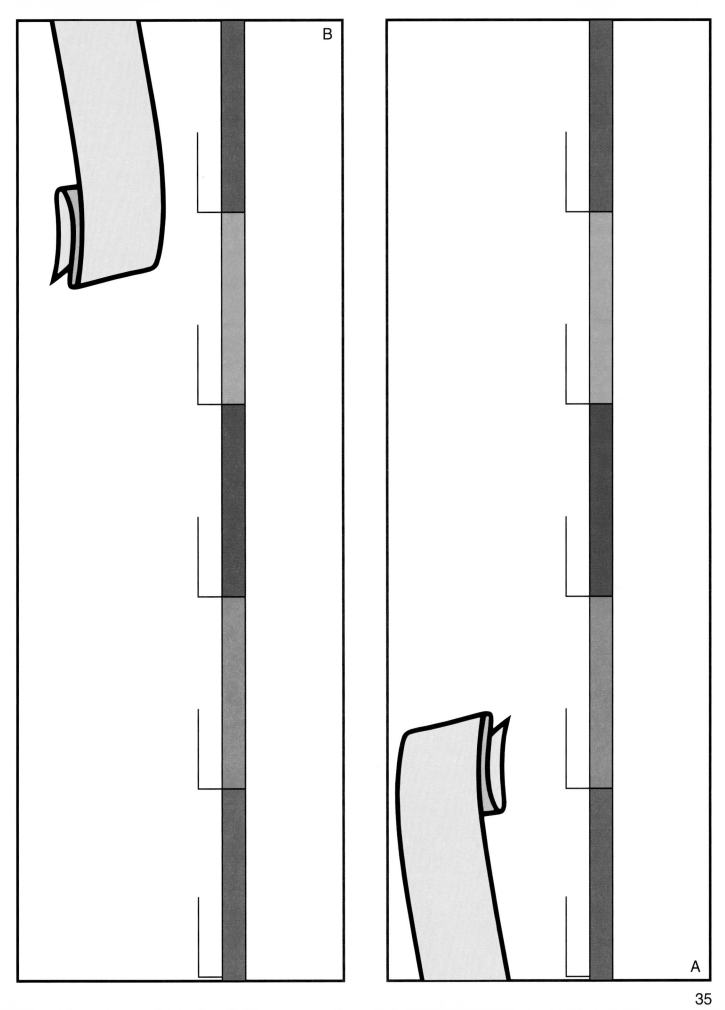

TIME CAPSULE

A time capsule is a container for putting away special things for a long time. You can make a time capsule about yourself. Write a message for your time capsule using any of these questions.

- What kinds of things do I do every day?
- What are some special things that have happened this year?
- What do I like to do best?
- Who are my best friends?
- What is my favorite food? song? book? sport?
- What are the best and worst things about my life now?

A Message to Myself

Date: _____

_____

_____

_____

_____

_____

_____

_____

_____

_____

_____

Choose some other things to put in the time capsule, such as pictures, poems, stories, song lyrics, or photographs. Place the message and other items in a shoebox, tape it shut, and label it as shown. Next year, open your time capsule to see what events the items help you remember.

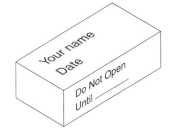

CRYSTAL CLEAR

In the 1500s, a doctor and scientist named Nostradamus sat down to predict the future. Staring into a candle flame, Nostradamus thought he could see visions of what was to come. He wrote down what he saw in mysterious poems. Some people who study his poems say that Nostradamus foretold true events, including the French Revolution and the invention of cars and planes.

What do you think will happen in the next century? In the crystal ball, write your predictions about any of the topics below.

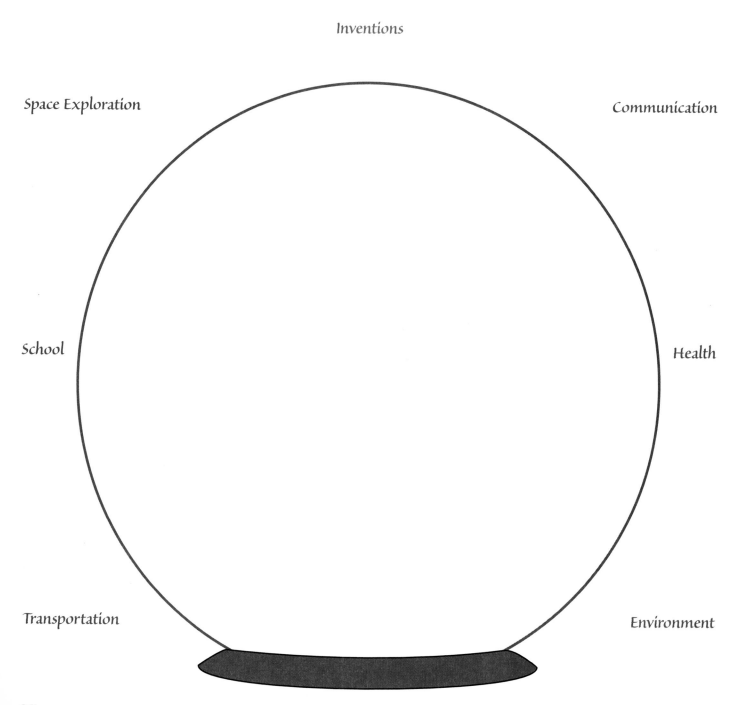

Inventions

Space Exploration

Communication

School

Health

Transportation

Environment

A MARTIAN CHRONICLE

Imagine that the year is 2130 and you are one of the first colonists on Mars. What will you miss the most about Earth? What will you like most about Mars? Write a letter to your friends back on Earth describing your new home. Use the facts about Mars below, to help you imagine living there.

Day Sky	Pale pink to yellow
Night Sky	Earth looks like a tiny blue dot. Mars has two moons: Phobos and Deimos.
Soil	Bright red to dark gray; rocky and dusty
Terrain	Flat plains, volcanoes, mountains, canyons, craters
Length of Day	24.6 hours (a little more than one Earth day)
Length of Year	About 686 Earth days
Gravity	38% of the Earth's gravity
Atmosphere	95% carbon dioxide; no oxygen
Temperature	-130°F to 65°F

Dear_____ ,   Date:_____

_____

_____

_____

_____

_____

_____

_____

_____

ALIEN LOGIC — Part 1

On Firstmonth 1, 2200, you leave your sleeping chamber in Compound 19 on the planet Alpha. Rubbing your eyes, you stumble into the kitchen. "Zzlgp!" a chirp greets you. You freeze, stare at the three visitors, and rub your eyes again.

Three aliens are sitting at the kitchen table looking at you hungrily. Your mind races. You know a lot about aliens, but can you remember who's who? Each alien is a different color. Each alien comes from a different planet. Each alien has a different favorite food.

Two of the aliens are shown below. In the box draw the third alien.

Use the clues on the next page to figure out the alien identities.

Zzlgp! (Hello!)
I am _____ .

Greetings, Earthling.
I am _____ .

CLUES

You know the following facts:

1. Quopik likes peanut butter.
2. Yoto is not from Orx.
3. The Zorgian is blue and likes peanut butter.
4. Grikba is not green.
5. The green alien likes marshmallows.

Use the clues above to complete the table below. Put a check (✔) in every box that is true, and a minus (–) in every box that cannot be true.

Alien's Name	Color			Planet			Favorite Human Food		
	Green	Blue	Purple	Orx	Glick	Zorg	Peanut Butter	Marshmallows	Pickles
Quopik									
Yoto									
Grikba									

Now label the pictures of the aliens and color the one you drew.

GROWING AND CHANGING

"The future is never carved in stone."

"There is nothing permanent except change" — Heraclitus

"Time is the greatest innovator." — Francis Bacon

What do these sayings mean? _____

_____

_____

You have changed in many ways since you were born. At this time in your life, what do you like about yourself? _____

_____

_____

How have you changed since last year? _____

_____

_____

What caused this change? _____

_____

_____

No matter how good or bad things are today, you can be sure that things will change. What would you like to change? _____

_____

_____

Can you make these changes? Why do you think so? _____

_____

_____

_____

NEW YEAR'S EVE

The world is divided into 24 different time zones. The time zones start at the Prime Meridian, the 0° longitude line that passes through Greenwich, England. Every 15 degrees west of the Prime Meridian is one hour earlier. Every 15 degrees east of the Prime Meridian is one hour later.

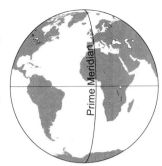

This map shows five time zones. The zones are not exactly within 15 degree areas because of political and natural boundaries, such as state lines and rivers.

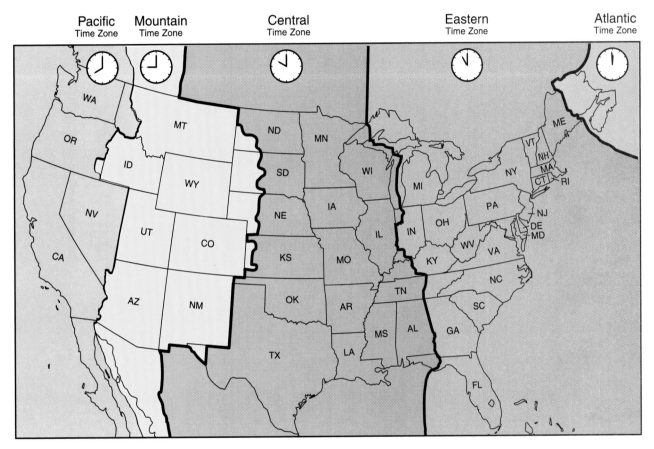

You want to telephone a friend to say "Happy New Year!" right at midnight where your friend lives. At what time and on what day would you call?

You are in:	Your friend lives in:	
	California (CA)	Illinois (IL)
1. New York (NY)	a. _____	b. _____
2. Texas (TX)	a. _____	b. _____
3. Colorado (CO)	a. _____	b. _____
4. Florida (FL)	a. _____	b. _____
5. Oregon (OR)	a. _____	b. _____

43

HAPPY NEW YEAR! — MAKING A CARD

All over the world, people celebrate the new year as a time of new beginnings. Choose your own language or one of the greetings below and make a Happy New Year card for your friend or family. Use the card-making instructions on page 45.

FELIZ ANO NOVO! — Portuguese
At midnight on New Year's Eve in Portugal, people go outside and bang pots together to signal the New Year. In Brazil, many people dress in white and eat lentils for good luck.

SHINNEN AKEMASHITE OMEDETOU GOZAIMASU! — Japanese
People in Japan clean their houses to start the new year off with a clean slate. Traditional foods, like sweet rice balls, are made and eaten for good fortune.

SHANA TOVA! — Hebrew
In Israel and other countries, Jewish people celebrate the new year in the fall. To make the new year sweet, they dip pieces of apple into honey.

GONG XI FA CAI — Mandarin
In China, firecrackers explode and a giant paper dragon dances through the streets.

AFE HYIA PA — Asanti
During the week of the new year, Ghanian families give each other gifts, such as goats, chickens, and ceremonial kente cloth. When you see someone for the first time in the new year, you say "Afe hyia pa" ("Welcome New Year"), even if it is October.

¡FELIZ AÑO NUEVO! — Spanish
In some places in Spain, people eat twelve big grapes on the twelve strokes of midnight, one for each month of the new year. In South American countries like Argentina, New Year's Day comes in the middle of the summer. People get together and barbecue, like a late-night Fourth of July party.

Use one of the designs below to make a Happy New Year card, or invent your own.

Book of Greetings

1. Cut an 8½ x 11 inch paper into four quarters.
2. Staple the pieces together along one side to make a booklet.
3. Write a new year greeting from a different country on each page.

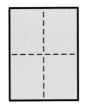
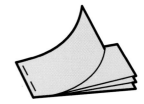

Opening House

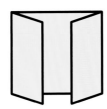

1. Fold a sheet of paper so that two flaps meet at the front.
2. Decorate the flaps to look like doors, and the inside of the card to show a home. Write a New Year's greeting on the inside.

Accordion Card

1. Cut an 8½ x 11 inch paper across the middle. Tape the two halves together.
2. Fold the strip to make an accordion-style card.
3. Write a different greeting on each section of the card, or stretch one greeting across the whole card.

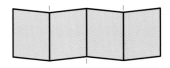

This card stands up for display.

Square Secret Card

1. Fold a square piece of paper in half. Then unfold it.
2. Fold it in half the other way. The folds will cross in the middle.
3. Open up the paper and fold each corner to the middle.
4. Write your message inside the flaps.
5. Use a sticker or tape to hold the corners together. Decorate around it.

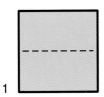
1

2

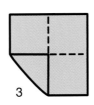
3

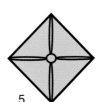
5

DO YOU KNOW THE TIME?

Time is so important in our lives that we talk about it all the time. Choose one saying and draw a picture of it in the clock.

1. Time flies
2. Time out
3. Time on your hands
4. Time's up
5. On time
6. Time is money

7. Take your time
8. Behind the times
9. The time is ripe
10. Killing time
11. Time marches on
12. Once upon a time

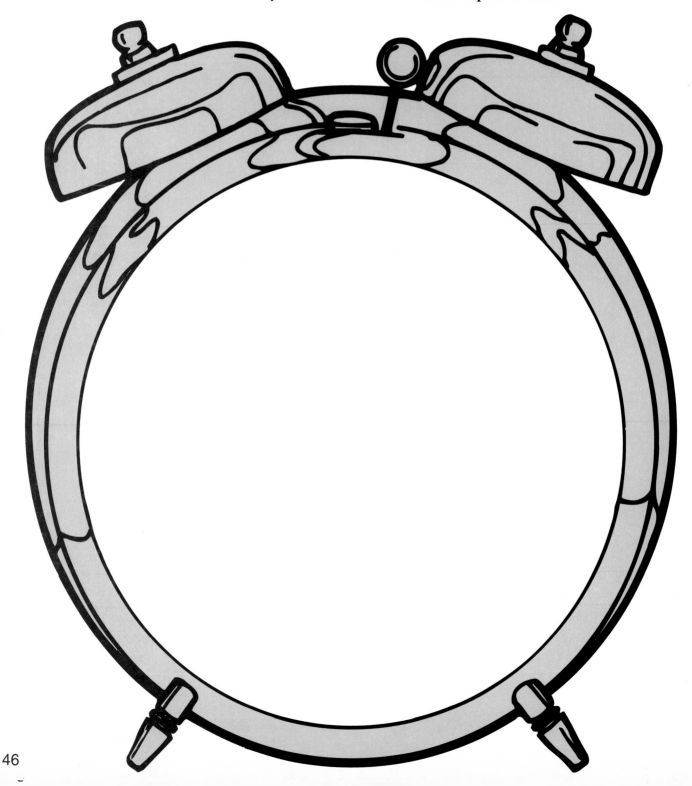

ANSWER KEY

page 5: A Clock in the Sky
The drawings should show the following pictures:

1. New Moon 2. Half Moon

3. Full Moon 4. Half Moon

page 6: Thinking About Time
1. Accept any device that measures time based on a regularly repeated interval, such as a digital clock, wall clock, or egg timer.
2. The moon changes in a monthly cycle; the sun rises each day; the stars move across the sky.
3. Some trees drop leaves in the fall; some animals migrate in the fall and spring; some animals hibernate or change color in the winter.
4. Answers will vary.

pages 7 and 9: Twelve Moons
Wolf: January   Buck or Thunder: July
Snow: February   Green Corn: August
Worm: March   Harvest: September
Pink: April   Hunter's: October
Flower: May   Beaver: November
Strawberry: June   Cold: December

page 11: When in Rome
1. April   2. October   3. June
4. January   5. July   6. August

page 12: How Many Minutes in a Millennium?
1. 1440 minutes
2. 10,080 minutes
3. 43,200 minutes
   (Months with 31 days have 44,640 minutes.)
4. 525,600 minutes
5. 5,256,000 minutes
6. 52,560,000 minutes
7. 525,600,000 minutes

ANSWER KEY, *continued*

page 17: **Geologic Logic**
From oldest to most recent: algae plant, trilobite, shark, first dinosaur, bird, last dinosaur, human

pages 20-21: **Rooted in History**
From a common root: milch, fleur, riviere, buch, couleur
Modern English words: friend/companion, wish/desire, room/chamber, smell/odor, answer/respond

page 25: **Measure for Measure**
12 ounces of spinach, 2 tablespoons of butter, ½ cup of currants, 3 tablespoons of vinegar, 32 sippets

page 33: **Getting Around**
1. horse, ship
2. early 1800s (Many historians give 1816 as the date for the invention of the bicycle.)
3. about 100 years
4. 1800s
5. Answers will vary.
6. horse, ship, bicycle, train, automobile, airplane, spacecraft

pages 40-41: **Alien Logic**
Quopik: blue, from the planet Zorg, likes peanut butter
Yoto: green, from the planet Glick, likes marshmallows
Grikba: purple, from the planet Orx, likes pickles

page 43: **New Year's Eve**

1.a. January 1, 3 am	b. January 1, 1 am
2.a. January 1, 2 am	b. January 1, 12 am
3.a. January 1, 1 am	b. December 31, 11 pm
4.a. January 1, 3 am	b. January 1, 1 am
5.a. January 1, 12 am	b. December 31, 10 pm

Note: When the Earth makes one daily revolution, it has turned 360°.
Each hour, it turns 15°.
$360 \div 15 = 24$ hours